A LIFE LIVED BEHIND GLASS

A Journey through the Autistic Spectrum

Marcie Layton

Huge Jam First Edition, 2021

www.hugejam.com

ISBN: 978-1-911249-65-8

Cover Image *"Towel Around Me" - mild steel wire, mixed media 143cm x 48cm*

Dedication

This book is dedicated to my wonderful husband Peter, and my two wonderful sons. They have been a constant support, and I love them immensely. I am proud to call them the Guardians of my Glass.

Acknowledgments

I would like to thank the all the specialists who have provided essential information and support, both privately and through the NHS. I list only their first names but they will know who they are: Bettina, Carolyn, Elin, Estelle, Kristina, Nolene and Olga.

Thank you to *Curtis Brown Creative* for their "Writing a Memoir" course, which helped me to begin learning the art of the memoir.

I also would like to offer my heartfelt thanks and gratitude to my longtime good friend Susan Peatfield, whose support and encouragement for my writing gave me the confidence to put my thoughts in print.

Jac Tobin, my editor, has been incredibly dedicated to the publication of this book. Her knowledge of publishing, and her sensitivity to my needs, have made the making of this book an absolute joy. This publication would not have been possible without her hard work and enthusiasm; I will be forever grateful.

Thanks must also go to Cecilia Gatehouse for granting permission to use a photo of one of her wire drawings as the image for the front cover.

Introduction

I LIVE MY LIFE BEHIND a wall of glass. It's not painful. It's not cold. I have clear visibility from every angle. But there is an unspoken distance between me and the people I meet, and nobody ever gets in.

Closest to me, but still outside the glass, are my husband Peter and my two boys, Dylan and Glyn. They are the guardians of the glass. They help me get through my life.

This is how autism feels to me.

Autism, or Autistic Spectrum Disorder as it's more formally known, is a developmental disorder that causes difficulties in communication and, often, a lack of empathy for other people. It can involve sensory difficulties as well: sensitivity to touch, light, sound and even to smell and taste.

The model of autism is often described as a spectrum, and there are a wide range of people on it; ranging from extremely challenged individuals with no language and low cognition, upwards to extremely intelligent people with off-the-chart IQs and awkward social skills.

It is said that all humans are placed somewhere on the spectrum. We're all just a little bit autistic. But in those people for whom autism is distressing, and alienating, life is a challenge.

I know now that I come from at least three generations of autism in my family, but this is comparatively recent information. I spent most of my life unaware of it, receiving an 'adult diagnosis' when I was in my forties.

My father was never diagnosed, as far as I know. But I recognise the indicators in him. My two older sisters have never said anything to me, so I'm not sure if they are affected.

There used to be a subset of the autistic spectrum known as Asperger's Syndrome, named after Hans Asperger, an Austrian paediatrician. Asperger's Syndrome was identified officially in the late 1930s and used to refer to those on the high end of the spectrum; those marked out through their extreme intelligence and poor social interaction. But today psychologists include Asperger's Syndrome within the autistic spectrum.

My father could well have been the Poster Child for Asperger's… Had he or anyone around him noticed his traits.

My glass wall feels safe for me, but I didn't ask for it to be there and I don't know what life would be like without it. I would be described neurologically as atypical, rather than neuro-typical, and I don't know what the glassless world of neuro-typical behaviour feels like.

We used to live in West London, in a large flat over Peter's drama school. It was an early Victorian building, with twenty or so rooms, bursting with noise and creativity. Our boys were both born in London, and our Welsh cottage, *Cwm Llan*, used only to be our holiday home. But as each holiday drew to a close, it became increasingly difficult to leave this cottage and its peaceful seclusion. We adored it.

Finally, when Peter retired from the day-to-day running of the school, we moved up here permanently, leaving behind us the noisy colourful clamour of London. We enrolled the two boys in the village school, which was a Welsh language school, began to learn Welsh ourselves, and started the process of adjusting to the rural lifestyle.

So, as if to shield me still further from the typical, we now live in a secluded cottage, Cwm Llan, which is in the hills outside Llangwm, a tiny hamlet smack in the middle of North Wales. I love the quiet here, and the peace. We're the only house in the valley (the cwm), and rarely have visitors. This house keeps my sensitivities calm.

Letting me write…

1

Life in Wales

"DO YOU THINK THAT YOU have an imagination?"

The therapist peered at me over his notepad.

"Excuse me? Do I what? Am I imaginative?"

I glared back at him.

"Do you feel that you have an imagination?"

"Um, well, I was a professional actor for thirteen years, in America and in London, and I teach and direct at a professional theatre school, so yeah, you could say that I have an imagination."

"Well, then you can't possibly be autistic. Autistic people have no imagination. They are too literal. I don't think that you're autistic."

He glanced down at his notebook and scribbled a few notes, then closed the book.

I just wanted to get up and punch him. Grab him by the scruff of the neck and shake the patronising bullshit out of him. What an asshole.

Instead, I just fumed silently, and politely extricated myself from the assessment as quickly as I could.

Back home, I was tearful and so confused. I didn't want to be autistic, no way. But if I was, then I wanted to know it, and for my autistic son to know it. I just didn't want him to feel lonely. And I wanted to make sense of my firmly held belief that my father was, in fact, undiagnosed Asperger's.

It's hard to explain why I would want to doggedly pursue a diagnosis which I didn't want in the first place. But just because I'm not aware of something doesn't mean it doesn't exist.

It's like the colour blue. I see blue, I recognise something which I call blue. But when you describe blue, is it the same as my blue? How do I know if your experience is the same as my experience? It's the same for atypical, and neuro-typical behaviour. I find something frightening. I feel lonely. I feel isolated behind an imaginary wall of glass. Is this the Human Experience? Or an autistic experience? I say I'm not good at maths. Is that because I'm not good at maths or is it because my autistic brain couldn't grasp the concepts when I was taught maths in a neuro-typical way? I just want to know if the things which I find challenging are the same for everyone, or if I need special help because they are only challenging for someone on the spectrum.

And my lovely lad, my beautiful little tow-head blond, who has grown into a tall, handsome young man with humour and charm, I just want Dylan to know that he is not alone in all of this. That his fears are my fears, and his confusion about some things is a legitimate confusion based on the fact that he is an atypical child trying to make sense of a neuro-typical world.

Life had begun settling down nicely after the first few months in Wales. The children were making friends, whose families in turn made friends with us. We began to form a picture of a future here and dared to daydream of our boys growing up happy.

But it all came crashing down when the school asked that our eldest boy Dylan take a hearing test. He'd never had a problem with his hearing before so I thought this was odd. They said he wasn't paying attention in class. I thought that poor attention in class could be from a variety of factors: poor visibility, uncomfortable seating, poor teaching, more interesting classmates, boring subject, the possibilities were endless.

I wasn't surprised when he passed his hearing test, but the headmistress wanted to explore further; she recommended that he see a child psychologist. I felt a bit worried about this, because I felt that there was nothing wrong with my son, it must be the school's fault that he wasn't paying attention. He'd been through so many drastic changes recently – new school, new classmates, new home, new language – it was understandable if his mind wandered.

Nevertheless we agreed and took him to a local CAMHS practitioner. She was a lovely woman, calm, plain-speaking, great with children. After our initial visit, she revealed what was actually going on.

"Headmistress asked for a hearing test," she told us, "but hearing wasn't really what she was concerned about. His lack of attention, she feels, might be something else entirely. She thinks that Dylan may be autistic."

"What?" I suddenly felt sick, scared, angry. "I don't even know what that is. Autistic?"

She could see blind panic on my face, and she continued, in a calm and reassuring voice.

"Autism is a developmental disorder which affects the way children communicate and interpret the world around them. It occurs..."

She stopped abruptly and reached for a tissue. She could see that I wasn't listening anymore, I was concentrating on trying to hide the fact that I was crying.

"Look, I know this is hard to take on board at first, and we have a few more tests to take to confirm a diagnosis, but I can send you home with some leaflets to read, and some good websites to look at. There is an organisation called the National Autistic Society which is an excellent resource."

But by then I was gone, just disappeared into my head, not listening anymore. There couldn't be anything wrong with my boy, he was perfect, he was gorgeous. We should never have left London, changed schools, moved to that crap village. What were we thinking, trying to teach him a new language? And who the hell were these people anyway, telling me there was something wrong with my son? I knew my boy better than anybody, there was nothing at all wrong with him. The teaching must be terrible, no wonder he couldn't concentrate.

"I must be honest with you," she said gently, trying to bring me mentally back into the room. "The hearing test is just a device to get parents to agree to have their child seen by a psychologist."

I stared at her. I felt tricked.

"If the teaching staff detect an attention problem, they try to eliminate a variety of possible causes, such as hearing, before looking at more serious options. I don't think the teachers at your school really felt that his hearing was at fault, they were just going through a series of procedures in order to arrange for him to be referred to me. Sometimes parents can - understandably - be concerned about what it might mean to be referred to a child psychologist."

"Fuck this," I thought, fuming inside. "I'm fucking going back to London. This is ridiculous. These people are fucking clueless."

I liked her, I really did, she was brilliant in the session with Dylan. So I couldn't possibly be mad at her. It was easier to be mad at the school, at the educational system, at the country, at the government, at anybody who dared tell me that there was something wrong with my lovely little boy.

I barely made it out to the car in a civil manner. Good thing Peter was driving. I tried not to show Dylan just how upset I was. He wasn't really interested anyway. He was happily off in a world of his own.

Autism. Huh.

I vaguely recalled having heard the word before, but really had to look it up in the dictionary. It wasn't a term that meant anything to me, and I'd had no experience of it before. But we agreed for him to be assessed by a child psychologist.

On the surface it appeared to be some sort of developmental disorder affecting his ability to communicate and process the world around him. I didn't recall this as having been a problem when he was younger but I didn't have anything to compare it to really, since he was our firstborn.

Thinking about it now, I recall that as a toddler, there was a long period when he didn't understand the word "I", and referred to himself as "you", because that was how we referred to him when addressing him. Then there was the time in London when the health visitor tested his vocabulary by showing him a drawing of vegetables:

"Now then," she said gently, "can you tell me the names of these vegetables?"

"Vegetables don't have names!" Dylan had shot back, scornfully.

Oh dear.

"My tummy's full of empty" he would say, looking hungrily at the biscuit tin. His comments made sense, but they didn't make sense. They made sense in another world, his world.

Sometimes, if he wasn't paying attention, I would say he was 'off on Planet Dylan'.

"Mummy?" he said one day. "Please don't say that. Please don't say I'm on Planet Dylan. It sounds lonely."

We had thought these cute little anomalies of childhood, anecdotes for the future, but now that the school was involved I beginning to get worried. Weekly assessments from the child psychologist gave us regular detailed reports from a one-to-one perspective. It was both fascinating and frightening – simultaneously.

Not surprisingly, the NHS services were overstretched in our area as elsewhere, and there were some long delays that began to panic me. We finally arranged for a private autism assessment in London, with shorter waiting times, in order to find out what was going on, and form some sort of a treatment plan as quickly as possible.

Watching the assessment was surreal. There was my son, sitting on the floor in the psychologist's front room, playing quietly, not unhappily, with me sat at the end of the room, seeing her watching him keenly and taking notes. There were quizzes and games and questions, and it all looked like a really jolly play date with the coolest toys in the world, but it was all forming a diagnosis in her head.

She confirmed a diagnosis of Asperger's Syndrome, and Peter and I drove solemnly back to North Wales, wondering what on earth we were going to do next. Autism can run in families, we were told, and we looked nervously at our youngest boy, Glyn, wondering if he was on the spectrum as well.

In retrospect, there were other elements going on in our lives which masked his symptoms. Moving away from familiar London, a new school, a new language, new friends, shyness, all these could have accounted for the difficulties he was having. Someone in his school in London had noticed that he played next to other children, not with them; one of several subtle differences, that had we connected the dots, would have added up to something more fundamentally serious.

Once, in his London primary school, he had been sent to the headmaster for being disruptive. He was feeling sleepy that morning, and the day started badly.

His form teacher rapped her desk for attention. "All right, children, settle down, please come over and sit here for Circle Time."

The young children dutifully went across to the carpeted part of the classroom and sat in a tidy circle. Dylan lay down on the floor, on his back. The teacher, looking mildly annoyed, glanced at him.

"Dylan, can you sit up please?" He looked up at her, baffled, and stood up.

"Dylan," she said again, tersely, "Please sit down." He lay back down on the floor. The children stifled giggles.

"Dylan. Sit up now." He wavered, confused and nervous, started to stand, then crouched, then stood up again, flushing.

"Right. Children, quiet please! Dylan, I would like you now to please go and see Mr. Brooks and explain to him why you do not want to sit quietly like the other children. I am not happy."

He slowly walked out of the classroom, his pale skin even more pale, his eyes beginning to well up.

We returned to Wales after the assessment with the London child psychologist, read up as much as we could, and began to wade into the deep waters of the autistic spectrum. Because the Welsh village school was so small, it was easy to watch him in class and help him if he needed it. But this was one of the challenges he faced: asking for help. He would sit and watch, but not be engaged. His mind wandered, and if he couldn't do an assignment he would just sit there, rather than asking for help.

We were advised to put him in the front row, so he would have no distractions between himself and the teacher, who was working directly in front of him. But he preferred to be in the back of the classroom, where he couldn't be seen, and it was a regular battle to get him seated where he needed to be. He had a little card that he was supposed to hold up if he needed help, but he never liked drawing attention to himself, and he didn't like people knowing that he needed help, so the card remained on his desk, untouched.

He became frustrated very quickly, had tantrums on a regular basis. As an adult watching his behaviour, you could see clearly, in any given situation, what the frustration was and his inability to master it. He wasn't a mean child, a bad child, a naughty child. He was a frustrated child.

An autistic child.

And so a Wall of Experience began to slowly grow up around me, a sharp-edged barrier reef. It was a wall between me and the other parents. And it was being built, brick by painful brick, upon experience: because I began to realise that my experiences of parenting were rapidly becoming different from those of most of the parents around me. Not all parents, obviously, as we were not the only parents with a child who had "additional needs", but because autism is a hidden disability, many of the behaviours that caused problems were due to a disability that others mistook for naughtiness. You can't protect them from criticism by sending them out into the world with a tee shirt bearing the slogan "*Please excuse everything I do, I'm autistic.*"

2

How to Build a Wall

WHEN I WAS MUCH YOUNGER, in California where I grew up, I began to feel isolated and alone. This was when I learned how to become a Wall Builder.

During my teenage years, my mother was dying painfully from ALS, Amyotrophic Lateral Sclerosis, a Motor Neurone Disease. Her body deteriorated for one entire year in ICU alone. It is an insidious disease, taking the body first and leaving the brain alive and kicking until last. It's often referred to as Lou Gehrig's Disease, after the baseball hero, but most people nowadays associate it with Professor Stephen Hawking, with his computerised voice and elaborate wheelchair.

It was the sort of situation where at random, over a long period of time, parts of her body would lose muscle strength. Sometimes she would lose control of a muscle, and then regain it again. Other times muscles would slowly begin to deteriorate and never recover full strength. Each isolated incident would seem odd, until connecting all the dots led to a diagnosis which nobody wanted to hear. During this time, I found it difficult to talk to my friends about what was going on at home. Everyone in my family was confused, and I was frightened. You could see the stress in my mother's face, increasingly worried about her deteriorating strength.

My mother was a tall woman, handsome and slim with beach-sand blonde hair and a warm smile. She descended slowly into a comatose invalid over about a ten-year period, succumbing finally when I was eighteen years old.

Once - I must have been about twelve at the time - we were driving down Pacific Coast Highway, came to a fairly steep hill. As we drove down it, my mother began to accelerate, rather than decelerate. I gasped. She stared ahead. The car raced on. I looked across at her. I panicked.

"Mommy, slow down please!" I gasped, clutching hold of the dashboard. Oncoming traffic veered away from us as we threatened the opposite lane.

"I can't!" she said, frightened.

I turned in my seat and stared at her. Her face was white, tense. She gripped the steering wheel tightly with both hands.

"Mommy! Please! Please slow down!" I cried.

Somehow, she managed to prize the fingers of one hand off the steering wheel, reach down, and actually lift her foot across from the accelerator to the brake. The car lurched, shuddered and careened violently over to the kerb.

When we were finally stopped, the car idling uneasily, she began to sob, deep gut-wrenching sobs. I had never seen my mother out of control before, seen her so terrified, so shaken. In fact, it was probably the first time I had ever seen her cry.

"Couldn't lift my foot," she managed to whisper, "I couldn't lift it off of the accelerator. My foot wouldn't work."

I have no idea how we got home. Probably retrieved by my dad. Somebody must have phoned him, but nobody had mobile phones back then so I don't know who. I was too young to drive. The car must have been left behind, on that steep hill. The logistics didn't matter. Bits were beginning to die in my mother and we needed to find out why.

Up until then we'd had a pretty wonderful quality of life. I wouldn't say my family had been composed of wildly active people, not exactly jetsetters. But life was good. You can see in old photographs that my parents were a happy and handsome couple: my slim, tanned mother smiles. My dad sits with his arm around her proudly. He had been a fit, young, dark-haired Navy man, and had now settled into the comfortable paunch and receding hairline of fatherhood. She kept her figure, a willowy and graceful woman.

They had made friends with three other couples, "The Bridge Group", and they were all very close. As was popular in the late 1960s and early 1970s, the wives had bridge lunches, wore sheath dresses by day and kaftans by night. I would arrive home after school and smell stale cigarette smoke (her friends loved to smoke) and old percolator coffee, see the remains of a great lunch in the kitchen, and know that this had been a Bridge Group Day. It made my mother so happy to have close friends. When I think of her now, if I'm not haunted by the image of her, comatose on a respirator, then I remember her tanned and healthy, wearing Capri pants, sitting on the kitchen counter in our old house, talking on the phone and laughing delightedly.

My dad was generous, shy and correct; he was also socially awkward and very honest. He could manage these friendships because my mother gave him access to them. The three other couples in the Bridge Group had invested in a Mexican time-share in Ensenada, a wonderful holiday house on the cliffs overlooking the sea. My parents, though not investors, were invited regularly. My father's contribution, by way of a thank you, would be to spend a substantial amount of time during these visits with his head under the kitchen sink repairing things, or looking at malfunctioning appliances, sorting the little annoyances of holiday living. He was happy to do it, and there was an easy balance among these four couples which sustained my parents and gave them joy.

My parents adored each other. They were mate-for-lifers.

I loved to watch my mother be happy with her friends. They would come back from weekends in Mexico with hand-painted pottery, embroidered summer dresses, silver and turquoise jewellery, plates and platters and crockery for the kitchen. Spanish style was very on-trend during this time, and we were far enough down the Southern California coast to make it a long, but not arduous journey.

The entire family went once, maybe twice. It felt exotic and privileged. I worried about drinking the water and worried about the food. Somebody told me that as you queued in Tijuana to cross the border people might break into your car, so you had to roll up the windows and lock the doors. Although this may have been true, the bad things never happened to us, and we were fine.

When my parents' world was safe, and secure and vibrant, I was safe and secure and vibrant as well.

We were a typical upper-middle class American family, with two cars, a dog, and an American flag displayed on the front of the house for national holidays. If we had carried on this way, lived our lives in the swimming-pooled-and-Country-Clubbed lifestyle of our peers, I wonder what we would be like today. I don't wonder in a despairing way, particularly. I'm just curious. I think about the road not taken.

These trips to Mexico were a rarity. My dad didn't really like going anywhere. After the Korean war, he had been on a goodwill tour with the U.S. Navy, and that gave him a chance to see the world. It probably never occurred to him that we would like to see it too. Many people on the spectrum crave routine and familiarity, and my father was no exception.

Every summer he would book a fortnight's holiday at a beachfront holiday home in San Juan Capistrano. It was pretty spectacular, and most of my happiest childhood memories took place there. Fortunately I loved those holidays and never minded the regularity of it all. I never questioned the fact that we never went anywhere else. That was the norm. Once I remember we went on a cruise to Alaska; I have no idea why. It was a little flash of brightness, this cruise, like a shiny bit of metal winking in the sunlight, but it was gone as quickly as it came.

I wonder if my parents had planned to travel more when their children were grown. They never got the chance. Things just didn't pan out the way they expected.

3

Living in a Glass House

OVER THE COURSE OF THE next year or so, investigations into my mother's condition began, sometimes locally and sometimes further afield, including a few visits to the Mayo Clinic in Arizona.

Kids at school were gossiping about boys, and dates, and clothes, and I had this daily hefty experience going on at home that none of my friends could relate to. I think I felt that if I confided in them it would be too great a burden for them to share. Or maybe I didn't have the skills to communicate to them what was going on..

They were just kids, after all. I was just a kid.

Uncertainty about self-sharing is one of the elements of autism. I would often fluctuate between over-sharing, and clamming up, and it was so difficult for me to gauge an appropriate response, so I don't recall ever discussing the situation at all with any of my friends.

Ever.

My dad was off-the-charts vulnerable, and fragile, and utterly busted up inside. It didn't feel safe talking to him.

Constantly, I could feel him just trying to keep it all together. As any parent would. But here I'm talking about an undiagnosed autistic adult, an only child who had gone through the trauma of his parents' divorce, and already seen his own mother die of leukaemia, when he was younger. So he must've had some serious wall-building skills himself.

I remember sensing, rather than seeing anger from him, much of the time. That awful way you can feel a thunderstorm, long before it arrives, just through atmospheric pressure. Many people on the spectrum feel uncomfortable looking other people in the face. This is really detrimental to communication skills, as it forces them to rely on other methods to interpret reactions and responses.

I can only describe it as 'noisy' for me, looking someone in the face. You can read so much information from people's facial reactions, it can be very distracting, especially if you are unsure about how you are coming across to someone. I can really get thrown if I look someone in the face, forget what I'm saying, lose concentration, feel shy, embarrassed.

I often forget people's names when I am first introduced. I'm too busy with a noisy inner monologue: "Wow, that person looks annoyed. They probably don't like me. Maybe they've heard about me from one of my neighbours. This guy looks like that actor in that Harrison Ford movie, oh what was the name of that movie...." So of course the name has escaped me!

When I was around my father, if I didn't look him in the face then I wouldn't have to see if he was mad, or disappointed, or whatever. But I could sense it.

He had a temper – I've inherited that unfortunately – but he was never ever violent. When he did blow, he would really blow, but it was verbal and it was frightening. He would bend, and bend, and then suddenly snap. I would never see his anger, because I chose not to look. I could hear it, though, feel it. The threat of anger alone would keep me in check.

I don't believe in astrology. Having said that, my dad was a Classic Taurus, and I was a Classic Cancer.

He found a variety of things to help him feel in control of his life. Keeping a tight rein on his finances helped him. Investing wisely but cautiously helped too. He became obsessive about doing his taxes each year. He hated the thought of giving even so much as a penny to the Tax Man, if he could avoid it. He became so obsessive that, in addition to not wanting us to bother him during tax time, not bothering him during the months running up to tax time became crucial as well. I'm stopping just short of saying he never wanted us to bother him because that's just not true. He loved to see us. In his way.

Bourbon and Coke, regularly administered throughout the day, gave him balance. He was never a fall-down drunk, he was a steady, balanced drinker. I think it might have had to do with his education and career as a chemical engineer. I'm sure this sounds bizarre, to a neurotypical reader, ascribing drinking habits to a career path, but it does actually kind of make sense if you think about it. He would never drink to lose control, he would drink to retain control, with a chemical balance of alcohol and sugar and caffeine throughout the day. On the rocks.

In our neighbourhood, it was assumed that everybody would go to college. So our grades were important. But our family's traditional model of mom at home, dad at work had been disrupted. With my dad close to breaking under the pressure, I tried not to let anybody know if I was doing poorly in school, because I didn't want help. I was very frightened of getting help with my homework anyway. For a child with undiagnosed autism, offers of help were a recipe for disaster, as I mentioned with regard to Dylan's schooling.

Maths and science were my bugbears, and of course my dad, being the brilliant maths and science guy, would have been the obvious person to help me. But because of his temper, he was also not the obvious person to help me. If he found out that I was failing, or even just struggling, we would sit down together and he would look at my assignments, and I would just sit there quaking inside, so frightened that he would get mad.

Instead of concentrating on the assignment, my thoughts were racing.

"Please don't get mad. Oh, he's getting mad. Oh *please* don't get mad at me, *please*."

I could feel him winding up, just like the approaching thunderstorm, and finally all I could think about was defusing that storm somehow. Much has been made about autism and poor communications skills. But it occurs to me that it relates to communication with neuro-typical people. I like to think that I can be very attuned to other people on the spectrum.

He would try to show me how to do an equation. I could feel him gather his thundercloud energy together and compose himself. Inwardly sigh. I could feel him instructing himself not to lose his temper, not to frighten me. Life behind glass!

Balancing my cheque book was the worst ordeal.

We would sit at the kitchen table. The California sun would bake us, fading everything in sight: the table, the chairs, the carpet. The hot Naugahyde chairs gave off a faint plasticky odour, and the back of my legs scorched as I took my seat.

"Okay, Marcie, may I see your cheque book please?"

I would hand it over, trying not to show my nervousness. He was a precise speaker, economical and careful with his words. This prolonged the agony.

"You haven't been recording your entries." His pencil would twitch. My throat would tighten.

"Why don't you record the amounts of your cheques? You need to do it every time you write a cheque! I keep telling you this!" I could feel the pressure rise in the room.

He would get a grip on his anger, will it to settle, try another tactic.

"Okay, we are going to need to fill in each of these entries before we can find the balance. Take this pencil please, and start here."

There were pages of unmarked entries. This was going to take a while.

I couldn't do it. I just couldn't do the sums. It wasn't lack of understanding. I was so busy concentrating on controlling my fear, I couldn't concentrate on the cheque book. I worried that if I took the pencil in my hand it would shake. So he would do the next sum for me. And then it was my turn.

"Okay, I'd like you to carry on just like this, fill in all of these unmarked entries, and then we'll go through them together. Come and get me when you're done".

I could hear him go off to the kitchen, hear the refrigerator door open, hear bottles and the clink of ice.

I would struggle, and shake, and try not to panic, and the tiny, pencilled numbers would float and wander around the page. Finally, an eternity later, I would bring the book to his desk. He would peer at me over his little store-bought half-moon reading glasses.

"Finished?" I would nod.

"Okay, let's have a look." He forced a smile, trying to look patient. He took the cheque book, scanned the entries, did the sums easily in his head.

"No, this one's not right." I held my breath. "Look here, these two don't add up." I couldn't concentrate. The air was getting heavy.

"You need to understand," he would explain tightly, "that if you are even one penny off, then your sums are wrong." He punctuated each word with a jab of the pencil on the desk. "Mathematics are precise. You can't be *near* the right amount. *It has to be the right amount. Precisely. Anything other than the precise number is a wrong number.*"

I wanted to cry. I held it in, and it hurt my throat and my eyes, and I could feel my heart pounding. If I was lucky he would give up trying to teach me, and just do the sums himself, me sitting next to him staring at the shag carpet and concentrating all of my energy on not crying.

I nearly failed chemistry. This must have cut him to the core. Only last-minute panic measures got me through.

Algebra was even worse. I took Algebra One and failed that and then I couldn't take Algebra Two until I'd passed Algebra One so I had to take Algebra One again while everybody else was taking Algebra Two and then I had to take Algebra Two, but I had to wait another half a term to take Algebra Two, so my dad, afraid that I would forget everything I'd learned in Algebra One, made me take Algebra One for the third time before I took Algebra Two.

I hate maths. Hate it.

Even now, in my 60s, if you give me any sort of math problem to solve I hear a tiny voice inside me crying "*Please don't get mad. Please don't get mad*."

In my first year at college my dad deposited spending money in my checking account. We discussed how much was in there, and he broke it down into weeks and told me precisely how much I could spend each week. I nodded and agreed and said I understood but I didn't because I wasn't listening; I was thinking about how to make sure he didn't get mad.

In the first flush of excitement at being in college, and in a dorm room, and a new town, and a town filled with university students, I went shopping.

I found the most exciting Army Surplus store near the campus. This would have been about 1978-9 so Army surplus was really cool. I remember leaving the shop with – among other things – the most exciting pair of faded, second-hand aqua coloured surgical scrubs trousers. I also bought a one-piece parachute flight suit, olive drab, with all sorts of zippers and pockets. The main zipper up and down the body of the suit was broken but I bought it anyway and held the thing together with a webbed army surplus belt. I would wear black high heeled shoes with it and a white tee shirt with a picture of Charlie Chaplin on it, and it was my most favourite outfit.

For many people on the spectrum, common sense is in short supply. That would be me.

The shopping spree in that one store alone wiped me out; I'd spent almost all of my first term's spending money, in one day, in the Army Surplus store. I put off telling my dad until I was totally skint. Luckily, when I broke the news to him I was on the phone, long distance, so I was safe from any increase in atmospheric pressure, but I could still feel the heatwaves coming down the phoneline.

Finally, in desperation, he sent me off one semester with a handful of brown envelopes, and I was honour-bound to divide up my term's allowance into the envelopes. I could only use one envelope per week. This worked, nearly. But I was always short by the end of term. So home I would go, at the holidays, with dirty laundry and no money and the fear about balancing my cheque book.

I'm sure that anybody reading this, in a challenging frame of mind, would say to me "How did you know if he'd get mad? How could you possibly know what he was really feeling?" Well, the answer is, I didn't know, and that was the problem. Autism limits my ability to gauge other people's emotions accurately, and if I don't feel comfortable looking people in the face, and don't have a viable emotional compass, then I can misjudge people and their actions. He was never, as I've mentioned, a violent man. The sheer willpower required not to lash out must have been tremendous. And this is what I could feel. The subterranean rumble of an angry man not acting out.

I feel so nauseous right now, writing critical things about someone that I love. But I'm only feeling sick because I cared about him and I feel guilty writing all about him, warts and all. He lived to a reasonably old age. Never re-married. He lived alone in a pleasant coastal two-bedroom house, with an alarming collection of old, yellowing Wall Street Journals stacked high in the bathroom.

He mellowed so much with age. He would still cook bacon until it burned (trichinosis was always a fear), and regulate himself with Bourbon and Coke, and not allow his routine to be interrupted even when he had visitors, but instead of deconstructing completely, he built a new him; he saved himself. He constructed a widower who lived peacefully in the memory of his beloved wife.

When he died, his final instructions were to have his ashes scattered at sea. He didn't want to be a burden to us in his old age, and he didn't want to have a gravesite which we would feel compelled to visit and maintain. As we sailed out that morning, on a large, hired schooner, leaping dolphins flanked his scattering, and led him to his new home.

4

The New Normal

I CAN'T REMEMBER WHY I chose a college so far away from my dying mother. It was in Northern California, about an hour's flight from my home. Choosing the right size of college seemed vital to me and I chose Chico State which was a middling sized school: not so huge as to be daunting, but big enough to have a decent Performing Arts department. It was never discussed that I wouldn't go off to school. I never considered it an option. If my parents discussed it they never let me know.

I was told, years later, that they had discussed between themselves how her final years might go, and how we, as a family, were going to cope. Apparently they decided, on my behalf, that we were to carry on regardless: go off to college, get our degrees, not interrupt our lives until our lives were interrupted for us. It seems that they also discussed having all of us just drop everything and be together for my mum's final year, maybe go off somewhere and do something together, but they decided against that.

I was so angry for years about this, because if I'd been consulted, I would have made that choice: to drop our lives and exit the mainstream for a bit, do something special together, all of us. But they had no idea how long she was going to live, and how debilitated she was going to become. So faced with such an open-ended question, carrying on regardless was probably sensible.

Back at High School, before things got really obviously bad, I began to discover that if I didn't talk about what was happening to other people, then it didn't exist. My new little toddler Wall of Experience was beginning to grow, encircling my immediate family, and keeping out everybody else.

This seemed to work for me. By the time I was about sixteen, I could go to the beach, and act in school plays, and play flute in the marching band, and I didn't have to address the deterioration, or the worry, with anyone on the other side of the Wall. If I kept my head down and didn't trigger my dad's temper, then it made things a lot easier. It was the least I could do for him. He was floundering, trying not to show it, but he really was.

Once the diagnosis came, and we realized the implications, we moved to a ranch style house all on one level with no stairs, and wide corridors for the eventual arrival of a wheelchair.

Word got out. I couldn't hide from the outside world what was happening. I was in a new town, meeting new people, trying to hide inside this little enclave I'd built, but of course people began to peer in. I guess we became known as the Family with the Lady in a Wheelchair.

Once, a new acquaintance of my mum's offered to make me a skirt. My mother used to love to sew, and now she couldn't, so the logic seemed to be that this woman would make a new skirt for me instead. I got to choose the fabric, and the pattern, and she was going to create this tailor-made little gift for me. It was such a kind gesture.

I was so angry.

I was so illogically, unreasonably, ungratefully furious at her, this kind and well-meaning lady. I could hardly bear to look at the thing.

However, it was soft, and flannel, with no zips or buttons, just how I liked it. It was a wrap-around waistline, full length, and actually rather like a big soft baby's blanket. And I did eventually wear it quite a bit.

But I was still, so so angry with her. Because sewing a soft little skirt for me didn't take the disease away from my mother.

As a teenager, huge hormonal waves of emotion were beginning to crash down on my head, (just like they were for everyone my age), but I wasn't prepared to deal with these big strong teenage feelings. Didn't have the equipment. Couldn't communicate what was going on inside. Didn't recognise that other teenagers my age were experiencing many of the same things. So the Wall got higher, while her symptoms got worse.

And the irony was, even though the Wall-building defences didn't serve me well as a teenager, I took to Wall-building again, years later as an adult, with my new neighbours and the boys' new classmates. It was the only way I knew how to cope. I think some people are condemned to make the same mistakes over and over again, as they have in childhood, unless they come across new information which can show them that here is another, healthier way to react to life.

As my mother's illness progressed, we had begun to settle into a new normal, where the curious looking medical accoutrements of terminal illness became ordinary. We now had a large van with a disability lift at the side. My mum had an electric wheelchair. There was a big, cumbersome hydraulic Hoyer lift with a sling for transporting her to and from her chair, and the toilet.

I have emblazoned in my memory the day my father was trying to transport her, in her sling, into a very small bathroom we had in the hallway. The corridors and hallways in our house were stylishly wide; the bathrooms were tight and mean.

It must be incredibly humiliating, being carted around in a sling. No privacy. No dignity. The simple act of going to the toilet would become a mini-event taking maybe ten, twenty minutes. I was never asked to help out with this sort of activity; showers and bathroom visits and general transportation were my dad's domain. I would disappear quietly until the awkward moment had passed.

But on this particular occasion it happened in the central hallway of the house. Something went wrong, it got stuck, maybe a strap got caught somehow, and my dad really struggled to make the thing move.

After a few minutes she'd had enough. She began to sob uncontrollably, hysterically, flailing her arms about weakly and trying, with her deteriorating fists, to beat away the confining straps. She was weak as a kitten; her body was just wasting away and she had no more effect on the restricting straps than the brush of a feather. My mind flashed back to the incident in the car, that same helplessness and hopelessness.

I shouldn't have seen that. She wouldn't have wanted me to see that, but I did.

The embarrassment, the frustration, the depression, the terror, the exhaustion: it was all there and I could see it, playing itself out in front of me.

We decided to get in part-time help for a while.

Pauline was a real piece of work. She was English, or possibly Australian, with an unnatural, leathery, mahogany tan. I hated the idea of having a stranger in our house, but the daily burdens my dad had to shoulder were beginning to take their toll. Her needs were becoming more sophisticated and it seemed to make sense. We wanted to keep her at home as long as possible, so I swallowed my annoyance and accepted her presence.

She didn't last long. My dad sacked her when he found my mum's pain relief prescriptions were going missing. There was an entire pharmacy of truly hefty medications in their medicine cabinet and she just helped herself, hoping nobody would notice. But my dad, precise individual that he was, did notice. She had a cock-and-bull story about having some sort of illness herself but honestly, I just didn't care. I didn't know what the alternative might be but I just wanted her out.

Over the next few years, I began to perfect this sort of split-screen lifestyle, leading the life of a California beach teen on the outside, and coping with family trauma on the inside.

But sometimes I let the outside, inside.

One day, when I was sixteen, it all got impossibly worse. There was a beach party going on, my favourite sort of party. It wasn't really a party, I guess, just a sort of get-together with food and stuff on the beach. I'd brought a brown paper bag filled with my favourite party food from the supermarket, and I arrived in a crapped-out Chevy Nova we'd inherited from my grandfather.

There was a guy there who I really had a crush on, and we all took turns jumping off the lifeguard's station, and nobody got hurt because it was just high enough that you could jump, and have a bit of flight, and then land with a light thud in the soft sand.

At this stage in teenage relationships, communication rarely takes place face-to-face, until something has actually been established. It might start with the traditional note passing in class, or glances across the gym during a basketball game. Usually the rumour mill started things going: some guy would whisper to some girl that his friend liked so-and-so, and that information would get filtered down either directly or indirectly to the recipient.

There was a girl in our music department named Imogen and she was perfect. She was a deep brunette, very curvaceous, and could wear cashmere jumpers next to her skin without developing acne. (I, by contrast, was tall and boyish. I was cast in my ballet school's production as Peter Pan, and was so flat-chested that Peter's boy costume fitted me perfectly…) It was just assumed that even if you liked a guy, they were all in love with Imogen really, so everybody else got hand-me-downs that Imogen didn't want.

This guy I really liked was in that category. He was tall, blonde, blue-eyed, with a little gap between his two front teeth, and goofy in a deadly attractive sort of way. I had resigned myself to the fact that he was one of Imogen's conquests, and I just needed to be content with gazing at him from afar.

But at the beach party, things changed. I heard from one girl, and then another, that it was possible that he liked me. That was the rumour. I was staggered.

I'd never had a boyfriend before. My first kiss had been a comedy kiss onstage in a school drama production. The thought that this guy, some guy, any guy, liked me, was unbelievable.

For children of the mobile phone generation, it is difficult to describe how different life was without mobile phones. No texting, no sexting, no Facebook, no Twitter. We talked to each other. Or gossiped.

But more to the point, for me, when I left the house for school in the morning, the only way my parents could reach me was by phoning the school. And whenever I was out and about, I was not able to be reached until I got home again. It made this separation between my home life and my public life very distinct. And trust between parents and their kids was crucial.

I was able to take a little break from my home life at this party, just concentrate on the delicious smells of the sea, and the crunch of potato chips, and the soft drink buzz, and the rush of adrenalin when I recognized the back of his head immediately when I got out of the car.

My deepest wish was that this guy would notice me. Maybe even say "hello".

I'd been glancing across at him during the party, watching everything he did, too nervous to go up and talk to him. We saw each other every day in music class, but I was in the woodwind section and he was in the brass section, so I never really got near enough to say anything.

Just towards the end of the party, as I was packing up to go to my car, I saw him look towards me. He began to pick his way carefully across the sand towards me, and all my fears and Imogenenvy melted away. I could see from his face that he was coming to talk to me. Me. It was all just so fun and innocent and sandy and fantastic.

"Hey, Marcie, wait up," he called out, breaking into a slow jog.

I turned and waited, heart beginning to pound. "Hi".

"Hi. Yeah, hi." He was slightly breathless, smiling.

"Hi."

"Um, you gonna, uh, d' you know about that thing in the drama department?"

"What, the movies?"

"Yeah."

"Yeah, we've decided to show movies in the theatre to raise money for our costume store. First one's on Tuesday." My toes curled slightly in the warm sand.

"Um, are you, um…" He stalled.

"We're showing *Butch Cassidy and the Sundance Kid.*" Good save.

"Oh, right, great, yeah, that sounds like a good one." He recovered.

"Yeah."

Pause.

"Um, maybe, do you want to, um…"

I looked down, too nervous to look at him.

"Uh," I fidgeted.

"Maybe we could go together?"

BANG.

I was floored. He asked me. He asked me out. I couldn't believe it.

"Yeah, sure, that'd be great. Yeah, thanks."

"Okay. Great. Uhh, great!" He looked down, shifted happily in the sand.

I stared at him, overcome. My bag of leftover party food was getting heavy. He glanced back up at me and I looked out to sea, watching the sun thinking about setting, turning pink and orange and golden, and flooding the beach with colour. I never wanted this moment to end.

"Yeah, thanks," I said, "I mean, yeah. That would be great. I gotta go, I'm so sorry, I said I'd be back."

"Yeah, no, I know, yeah, okay that's fine, that's okay."

"I'm sorry, it's just..."

"No no, it's okay, I'll be going soon too, I gotta work tonight anyway."

The whole of the beach was golden now, shining, bathed in happiness. I didn't want to go. My arms were aching but I didn't care; I could've stood there, just looking at him, forever.

"Okay, then, see you tomorrow, see you. Bye." I gave him a little wiggle of a wave with the hand gripping the paper bag.

"Bye." He grinned. I met his eyes, briefly, saw pure happiness. Blushed. Looked away.

"Okay then, bye. Bye."

Somehow I made it to the car, the shopping bag beginning to tear underneath. I was smitten.

It was a little conversation, inconsequential, just party chat. But I knew, I could sense it, that he had made some sort of ring road around Imogen and had decided that I was the one he was going to pursue.

I had a boyfriend now. And I just felt like a million bucks.

It killed me to leave, what with all this romance flying about, but I needed to go home. My parents trusted me to be home when I said I would be and I wouldn't consider violating this trust. I left quickly. I had to get home before dark. My thoughts were full of love and dreamy beach sunsets.

As I drove down the street towards our house, I could see lights flashing, and a large ambulance parked in front of the house. I felt sick with the adrenalin surging in me, curdling with the other adrenalin I'd been feeling from my encounter at the beach.

By the time I got to the house I could see both front doors wide open, which was odd. We never normally had them wide open like that except to bring in the Christmas tree. I could see medical staff in the hall with a stretcher. They were quickly wheeling my mum down the hall. She was wearing an oxygen mask and I could see her eyes above the mask, terrified, as she passed.

I was in full on panic mode, trying to figure out what had gone on while I had been larking about at the beach.

I think she had some sort of, I don't know, collapse maybe, or seizure, or maybe couldn't breathe. Anyway my dad had obviously called for an ambulance and they were rushing her off to the ICU.

I think now how curious it was that I started my first relationship on the day my mother went into hospital. Two monumental events on the same day. My personal life clashed with my social life.

Because the same thing happened again a few years later. In the same year in which my mother died, I had sex for the first time. With a boy I thought I was going to begin a relationship with. It turned out he only wanted a one-night stand. I felt rotten. Humiliated. I'd been "saving myself for marriage" as they say. But I think in that year, I decided that nothing really mattered anymore.

Loss became a way of life.

5

Hospital Life

MY MOTHER NEVER CAME HOME after that. She went straight to the ICU and stayed there until she died about a year later. My dad, ever the sensible one, had taken out some sort of major medical insurance that only kicked in when your medical bills topped one million dollars. Well, I think we claimed on that policy within a week, but amazingly, they honoured the policy and supported her medical treatment. You almost never hear of that happening, so we were incredibly lucky.

There were so many different ways in which she was being kept alive artificially. For a period of time she could still speak, and then when her vocal cords went she had an artificial vocal cord machine, a little handheld thing that you held up to your larynx, which allowed you to speak with a sort of computerised sound. When her arm muscles went, we held it for her. When her lungs failed she went onto a respirator, and the tracheotomy went in, and that little device was useless. There was no speaking going on after that. Finally, she was comatose and reliant entirely on life-support machines.

New normal, new normal, we were just trying to keep up with it all.

One of my sisters and I finally both got jobs at the hospital so we could spend more time with her. I worked in the dietary department, wheeling round hospital food to hungry patients, and not-so-hungry patients, who often couldn't stomach it.

There was a delightful, funny chef in the kitchen named Frank, big guy, who taught me how to crack eggs simultaneously in both hands. I was able to practice this while making up enormous vats of scrambled eggs. When I first tried it, I spent more time picking bits of shell out of the mixture than I did cracking the eggs, but as I practiced more, I finally managed four eggs simultaneously. This was incredibly satisfying. Even today when I crack eggs I think of Frank.

I think he was a New Yorker. He would make huge vats of delicious smelling food down in the kitchen, but by the time it was portioned out into little ceramic dishes, cling-filmed, and stacked into a tall trolley with a wobbly wheel, it had lost its charm. The Soft Food Diet patients suffered the most. There were scenes in which food was hurled across the room. It always turned out to be the Soft Food Diet trays. The fun trays I seem to recall were usually the T & As, the Tonsillectomies and Appendectomies. These were trays with Jello and ice cream. The Tonsillectomies were usually kids, and they didn't stay long, so there were always little unopened tubs of Jello and ice cream in the ward freezers, which were greedily gobbled by us between rounds.

I paraded around the hospital in a little white polyester uniform, and white nursing shoes with a thin slick of kitchen grime on them. I had begun to experiment with makeup by this time and must have been a curious sight indeed: a young teenager in neat white uniform and thick layers of foundation, mascara, blusher and lipstick.

I could see my mum all the time, and as a long-term resident she had special perks. Once we smuggled our new puppy in to see her, in a large wicker laundry basket. I was quite worried about doing this, because the rooms in ICU must be kept scrupulously clean and hygienic. I was worried that the puppy might contaminate her. But my dad said it was okay.

What hadn't occurred to me was that - because she was so ill - contamination from a little puppy wasn't going to make any difference. She was terminal, and it just didn't matter anymore. Keeping her spirits up was more important. We stood in the elevator, petrified with naughty fear, hoping not to get caught, and giggling with nervous excitement. If I'd actually looked at the nurses' faces on the ward, I would have noticed that they weren't angry at all. They were revelling in the naughtiness. But I never looked at their facial expressions, so I missed it.

She grinned weakly at the puppy, who we struggled to control, and this little burst of life and wriggliness and fun was just the perfect antidote to the sterile, medical world she lived in.

We brought in pretty pillowcases, and audio tapes, and tried our best to make the room homey. The hospital was situated on the Pacific Coast Highway with lovely views out to sea, so if you ever had moments of wistfulness, or melancholy, then you could just sit and look at the ocean until you felt better.

It was a strange sort of half-life, this time spent working at the hospital. It was a new normal that lasted for nearly a year, and even though her body was continually deteriorating, I'm not sure I really dwelled on the fact that one day she would die. Even though I was surrounded by hospital life and patients and medical staff on a daily basis, I just didn't think about her being dead. If an image came into my head I would block it out.

I'm sure that sounds incredibly naïve, but I think after all the upset and the changes and the series of "new normals" which we had been through, it just didn't seem right, or fair, to have her actually die at the end of all of it. It was almost as if, if we all coped and behaved ourselves, then she would stay alive.

But she did die, finally, when I was eighteen. Early January, when everybody was together for the Christmas holiday. I've been told that people often die around the holidays, or just after, when family and friends have been visiting, and unwittingly saying their last goodbyes. I remember very little about it. I've been assured that it's possible to awaken the memory of that time but I don't really see the point.

I'd been to have a haircut, and then went on to choir practice. I so very nearly went to the hospital first, after the haircut, but I was running a bit late and I didn't want to rush my visit, so I decided to go to choir practice first, have a longer, unhurried visit with her afterwards. I got a phone call at choir practice, asking me to go straight home. So I missed it.

Perhaps it was just as well.

She had been in a coma for quite a while, so it's not like, if I'd been there, I could have said goodbye. I was at university by this time and no longer worked at the hospital. The nurses told me that she could hear what people said, even though she was comatose, in the room and that I should talk to her.

I never knew what to say. At eighteen, a one-way conversation is very difficult.

I can remember vividly a birthday party I had when I was seven but I can't remember her death. I know that we had to all go together to pick out a coffin and that they were made of different materials, and they were different prices. I remember how difficult this was for my dad. I watched him try to decide. He was not a religious man and I wouldn't have dared to ask him his beliefs about the afterlife. I just think for a man like him, trying to put a price on his feeling for my mum, interpreting it in a choice of coffin, was just gruesome.

I think my dad chose Schubert's *Ave Maria* for the funeral service. It was probably recommended to him by someone at the funeral parlour, because he wasn't at all religious. He had been the most amazing classical pianist when he was younger but had lost the love of playing.

It doesn't upset me if I hear *Ave Maria*. I have no memory of the funeral, so when I hear it I just hear music, I don't feel anything. My heart has a sort of protective glaze over it, for memories like this.

She's buried somewhere in Southern California. I never visit the grave. I don't see the point. It was a place I didn't know, which I'd only visited on the day of the funeral, and it didn't have any significance for me. I suppose it would be nice to see her name carved in stone, but frankly I doubt if I could bear it.

So, we brought the nice pillowcases home, and the cassette recorder, and I don't think I ever set foot in that hospital again.

Periodically throughout my life I read about, or hear about, other people's tragedies. I read about childhood trauma. I hear about PTSD. I think about myself and wonder if I fit into that category. My mother would be the first to wear the badge of trauma. My father next, because he wasn't raised with so much as an ounce of coping mechanisms.

So many people have lived lives far more painful than my own. I just think of the events that occurred to me as My Life. I don't quantify it as being a sad life, or a happy life. So why do I sit here, decades later, streaming with tears as I write about something that happened to me when I was a teenager?

I am not holding onto these memories through choice. I have events from my younger self which are like the threads on a loom. They are literally the fabric of my life, and some of the threads are very dark. I have not snipped the threads and tied them off and carried on making the fabric with new colours. I still have the dark colours, and the light colours, from my childhood, and I carry on with the same colour scheme. Only the pattern is different.

6

The Woman Who Was My Mum

MUCH TO MY REGRET, I never got to know her as a woman, only ever as Mum.

I haven't intended to write about her as if she was a saint, because of course she was a flesh and blood woman. I just genuinely can't remember anything bad about her. If you asked me to pick out a character flaw, I would only be able to come up with something like "too kind".

I think about stuff like this a lot. Sort of like a theory of personality. Am I describing a well-rounded person to you if I don't describe their dark, as well as their bright, side?

I know how easy it can be, to put our departed loved ones on a pedestal. I love my mum. I love my dad. He's dead now, but I can describe how frightened I was of his temper and I can also say that I loved him. I can describe his bright side, as well as his dark side. I just happen to believe that my mum was a truly lovely human being. Isn't it encouraging to know that people like this do exist in real life, and not just in fairy tales?

I was too young to reach the equality of Womanhood with her. Just at the age when perhaps we might have been able to have womanly conversations, the illness took over and there were more important things to consider.

She had tried for a while to keep up her appearance. She wasn't a vain woman – she was actually incredibly modest - and trying to keep up her appearance was her way of keeping the encroaching disfigurement of ALS at bay.

Some hairstyles in the early seventies required a bit of work, often involving large rollers and back-combing. I think for a while we had a hairdresser come to the house. Her hair, in addition to the fresh sandy blonde colour, had an elegant natural wave in it which has been passed down through our family. My maternal grandmother used to Marcel hers, and my mother used to style hers, and I have my own natural wave as well (unstyled, dishevelled, but still waving). Dylan, our eldest, has it too, although he keeps his hair cropped short for cricket season. Sometimes in the wintertime he lets his hair grow long and wild, and I see my mother's wave in him, flopping casually across his forehead. I love seeing it: my mother's wave. But once the cricket bats come out, it gets shorn. Glyn has my father's hair, lots of dark hair, like a mop. I try not to annoy him but I do love running my fingers over it when I think he won't notice.

Something in her died the day she gave up styling her hair.

A few times she asked me to do her makeup. I would lean in towards her face, holding my breath, hand shaking, with a small eyebrow pencil or an eyeshadow brush, and cautiously try to use skills which I had not yet learnt for myself.

She used to tell us about the days when she and my father were courting, and how they went sailing on his beloved boat, *Slipstick*. My father had been in the Navy, and his wooden sailboat, a Thistle, was very important to our family.

He sold it when my mum fell ill. I think the joy left him. I'm sure it felt wrong to him to sail in it without her.

In preparation for their dates together, my mum would style her hair and set it with clouds of hairspray. As was the fashion of the day, she would carefully apply black mascara and a strong red lipstick, and a discreet dab of her favourite *Chanel No. 5*.

But the cosmetics of the early 1950s had none of the waterproof qualities which we have today. Off she would go to meet my dad for a sail, perfectly coiffured and made up. But after only a few minutes on the boat, the makeup would run, her hair would straggle, and all the careful work of the morning would be lost at sea. She came back bedraggled and delighted, tanned and in love. At sea they were very genuine with each other. I think this broke down barriers, and my father's shyness. It gave him an activity – like the kitchen sink repairs in Ensenada – and allowed him to share time with my mum minus the social awkwardness.

She was a kind, giving person and he was a shy and awkward man. She was very ladylike - the last of her friends to stop wearing white gloves and pearls for social occasions - and he was a very polite man, very correct, the sort of man nowadays we would probably label "a bit square". They fitted together like links in a chain, a hand in a glove.

It feels so strange for me to be a woman in front of my boys now, not just their mum. They see me drink wine, and swear, and lose my temper, and I feel so vulnerable, since I never had that experience with my own mum. They know my personality flaws now: they see me make bad decisions, and have doubts, and cry, and they make their own judgements about the world around them, not the judgements and opinions that we, their parents have made and imposed upon them. I realise this is the important stage of their growth and development as young men, and I only hope that as they discover who their parents really are, they will still like us, and love us, and forgive us our faults as they become grownups themselves.

So many children don't. Forgive.

7

Living with Special Educational Needs

SO, THIRTY OR SO YEARS later, in Llangwm, the new little wall that I'd been building around my parenting got higher and higher, but not necessarily stronger, in the way that if you stack bricks on top of each other very very high, but only one brick deep, then they are likely to sway and collapse.

Our youngest boy Glyn was also assessed for autism but was not considered to be on the spectrum. And yet he had developmental disorders of his own – with a few crossovers to autism – and just as we were beginning to get a handle on the first diagnosis, this second diagnosis came hard on its heels. It felt like being pulled under by a huge wave at the seaside, and then just as you struggle to come up for air a second wave knocks you broadside and takes you down again.

Despite the benefits of our little rural school, I just felt that the resources required to work separately with our two boys and their difficulties were going to be a burden to the school. And looking at it from the headmistress's point of view, it must have been quite challenging for her not only to integrate two English speaking boys from London into the school, but then to adapt their education to accommodate their special needs. It really wasn't fair on anyone at all.

I felt stressed, I felt awkward. I would fluctuate wildly between aggressive and despairing. We didn't want to move back to London, and it was unfair of me to be so demanding at the little school, and all the little markers on Dylan's desk, and revised seating plans, and SEN Statements from the local education authority were just not working.

I began to feel very low. The child psychologist described this feeling as similar to being in a well: just as you think that you are rising to the surface and climbing up out of the well, the second diagnosis pulls you down under the water again.

The oddest things would set me off; I felt rather fragile during this time.

One time we were at the Bethesda cricket ground: bright, sunny, with gorgeous mountain views. But I wasn't feeling sunny, or bright, because the process of a child's autism diagnosis is a long one, and it had sent me into a downward spiral.

I felt like a threadbare rug.

For weeks I had been argumentative with teachers, scrappy with parents, hypercritical about everybody else's parenting skills, because I was so desperately trying to cling to skills of my own. This week I had emotionally flatlined, and the only thing buoying me up at that moment was this little Junior cricket match, and my little lads in white. Cricket is an incredibly long game, but when my little lads were playing, I could watch for hours, no problem.

A steady stream of Welshmen had been filing into the community centre, unnoticed by me. Suddenly, a choral wave swelled and washed over me: a male voice choir rehearsing Ravel's *Pavane for a Dead Princess.* It was real lump-in-the-throat stuff, an incredibly tragic sound, and an odd counterpoint to the little match I was watching.

Suddenly it occurred to me: *I was the Princess. I was the fucking dead Princess.*

Me, with my airs and attitudes about what makes a good family and a good parent and good behaviour, and there I was with two children with Special Educational Needs and I was human, and just like everybody else, and we were all in the same boat, and there was nothing special about me at all and there I was just like a dead princess.

My heart began to pound and I could feel a panic attack drowning me but I couldn't tell anyone about it because then I'd have to explain why and I couldn't because I just couldn't see anybody understanding why I was feeling like a dead princess at a Junior cricket match in Bethesda.

So we decided to Home Educate.

And suddenly the sun came out, and the birds began to sing, and little cherubs fluttered around our heads playing musical instruments, and somewhere a heavenly choir began to sing, and we skipped and danced, hand in hand, grasping daisies and buttercups, and All Was Right with the World.

8

Home Educating

NOT EVERYONE IN OUR FAMILY thought home education was the right thing to do. I'm not sure if Dylan will ever be convinced. But as parents we need to do what we feel is in the best interests of our children and I had no qualms about the decision to pull the boys out of mainstream education. I'd do it again in a heartbeat. None of us will ever know how they would've coped if they had stayed in mainstream – we can only speculate – but from the amazing young men they have grown up to be, I'm certain that home education helped them to become who they are today. The advantages of this type of education, for our children with their needs, in our living situation, far outweighed the disadvantages. But we certainly didn't make the decision lightly; we did our homework first.

Home educated children learn faster, because they have fewer distractions and are more focussed. So, home school starts later and finishes earlier. Longer lunches. No school buses. No waiting around for thirty bits of paper to be passed around the classroom to thirty different students. No distractions from boys in the back row throwing spit wads. No unnecessary repeating of instructions for someone who wasn't listening, when you got the instructions the first time. And the freedom to have the instructions repeated if you yourself didn't understand them, without other children giving you grief. The freedom to go back over something if you didn't understand, without holding up the rest of the class. Subjects taught in a way that is accessible to your unique method of learning. No Assembly. No boring reading of the register. No school uniforms. No school shoes. No brown bag lunches. No smelly toilets. No bullying on the playground. No homework. Being allowed to do what you want during breaks and lunchtimes.

It's just a different world.

We decided to find an online curriculum for the 'spine' of our programme, and then flesh it out with specialist classes for our boys' Special Educational Needs.

We chose *Primary Home Education*, a programme which we bought online. When they reached high school age, we moved onto *The Chalkface Project.*

Cwm Llan has a dedicated dining room with a big extendable oak table. This was The Classroom. We also used a separate sitting room, so that each boy could go off with a separate teacher into a separate room. They rarely had classes together because they were two years apart. School trips were all taken together.

I managed to find a wall display which featured the days of the week on little placards. Each day of the week had its own little blackboard, on which the daily schedule was written, and we hung this across one wall of The Classroom. I devised a colour-coded system with chalks, which outlined who was doing what, and when. This worked well for us, for years, with slight modifications. This was how an average school day looked:

Class one:	10.00 – 11.00
Break one:	11.00 – 11.30
Class two:	11.30 – 12.30
Lunch:	12.30 – 13.30
Class three:	13.30 – 14.15
Break two:	14.15 – 14.30
Class four:	14.30 – 15.15

If there was an extra-curricular activity, such as football or cricket, then the boys would have a class free during the school day, and the extra-curricular class would be counted as a P.E. class.

I'll never forget the day our Primary Home Education materials arrived. It was like Christmas in the house. It was an enormous package filled with the most exciting looking educational tools: big beautiful, illustrated books of children's stories, brightly coloured science tools and equipment, magnets and cables and metal ball bearings and Perspex science goggles, course books and bright blue logbooks, and some items about which I had no idea, but which turned out to be mathematics tools. We were very strict about logging the day's activities, and these logbooks were laid out for the inspector during his annual visits.

Peter and I divvied up the classes between us and hired part-time help as well to share the load. Peter was retired, and I was a full-time mum, so we were able to dedicate our time completely to our boys' education.

It was a thrilling time. We discussed which subjects we personally felt we would like to teach the boys. Peter taught American and British history – including the American presidents and British prime ministers – and Shakespeare. I taught cookery from different countries, specifically Italian, French, Chinese, and American, and soprano recorder for Glyn, to help his fine motor skills.

I owe nearly everything I know about text and language to Peter. My generation was not a particularly articulate one. We were beginning to be distracted by video and mobile phones and the Internet, and our patience with the written word was limited. We were becoming a visual generation.

But Peter comes from a different era, where language is savoured, and in particular the works of Shakespeare. His school, Drama Studio London, is a post-graduate level professional actor training programme, which he founded and ran until his retirement in 2003. He trained at the Bristol Old Vic theatre school, and even to this day he will come across former classmates on telly and on stage. He used to fascinate students in his Shakespeare workshops, analysing the old fashioned and complex text, making it accessible to a modern audience. He has the gift of finding communality in Shakespeare and contemporary life, highlighting the fact that the feelings and actions of people in Elizabethan times are just as relevant and real in people living today.

When we first started teaching, I was very anxious to keep the school day regimented and on schedule. I didn't want the boys to think it was all playtime, or that they were bunking off education. We were answerable to the Conwy Educational Authority and would be subject to an annual inspection. We kept strictly to the class timetable; the boys were very good about coming in from breaks on time. I also think they appreciated the late starts.

After a while, as we settled into the regimen and the boys began to flourish, Peter and I began to be more adventurous in our concept of education. PHE had regularly scheduled outings, mostly for science and nature projects. But Peter and I began to look at the bigger picture, really opening up the subject matter for the boys, and relishing the fact that we were essentially introducing our boys to The World.

We didn't just read about Italy; we went to Italy. And America. And France. We didn't just read Shakespeare, we went to productions, designed costumes, learnt character analysis. Glyn had private singing lessons, performed in concerts at a local music school, recorded a solo CD before his voice broke. Dylan played as much cricket as he could possibly fit in - for both Junior and Senior teams - and qualified as a Junior coach from a young age.

If you look at the world around you as a big classroom, then everything you see and experience has a potential value. I like to think of education as a giant hors d'oeuvres platter: a wide variety of experiences and subjects for children to try, in order to help them towards their chosen careers. The more eclectic the ingredients on the tray, the wider the selection will be, and the more informed their choices will be, about what interests them. Some subjects might be tasted and spat out; other subjects might be gobbled greedily.

When we took our boys to visit my dad in California, I like to think that my dad inspired an early love of learning in little incidental ways. He loved meeting Dylan and Glyn. We rented a fabulous house on the beach for a fortnight, in precisely the same road where our family had spent happy summers all those years ago. One morning he told the boys he had something special he wanted to show them. He wanted them to have something passed down, from him.

He took us out to the patio, with the waves crunching in the distance, and he taught about his vision of chemistry. He gave both boys a little fridge magnet with the periodic table of elements on it. I braced myself for a chemistry lecture, but a new version of my dad appeared. He gently explained to my boys that what he found so exciting about chemistry was that everything in the world is chemistry.

He patted the wooden patio table. "*This is chemistry,*" he'd say, "a chemical reaction between elements, which creates wood."

He waved his hand around us. "The air is chemistry. This drink is chemistry. You are made up of chemistry. Everything in this world is made up of chemistry, and every element that makes up everything in this world is on the periodic table of the elements."

His eyes lit up as he described his passion, and I wasn't frightened, listening to him now. He adored his grandsons; I could see that. And at the end of his chat, while the boys got down from the table clutching their little fridge magnets and grinning, that day in particular I felt the balance restored between my dad and me.

The boys' education was practical and surreal in equal measure: exotic toys, exotic games, exotic exercises that all somehow added up to a very special world of learning, for our very special boys.

The Science and Nature curriculum was supplemented by DVDs such as *Wild China*, and Brian Cox's *Wonders of the Solar System*. We learned History of Music from an online radio programme: *Classics for Kids* with Naomi Lewin, and the boys played a child-friendly computer game which taught typing skills.

Our local vicar came up with an inspired idea. She came to the house weekly and taught Religious Education, in fun and creative ways. They went to church services, made harvest festival boxes for charity, visited the Stations of the Cross in Holywell.

One of our tutors taught drawing to Dylan, but origami to Glyn, which helped develop his fine motor skills. We had classes dedicated to brain-developing games like chess, or specialist board games like *Rush Hour*, which helped them both to plan ahead, and organize their thoughts.

I decided that not only would we research and celebrate traditional holidays, but we would research holidays and celebrations from foreign countries as well. On Shrove Tuesday, for example, instead of pancakes, we made Venetian Carnival masks and prepared an Italian feast; the next year we celebrated Mardi Gras with Cajun food. For Chinese New Year we made Mongolian Hot Pot. We celebrated American Fourth of July and Thanksgiving, in addition to British Boxing Day and May Bank Holiday.

PE was a challenge, but we came up with an eclectic mix. Cricket was a key part of their lives and being members of the local club helped them to develop social skills and teamwork. We took them off for swimming, tennis, and squash, and both boys joined the local squash club. If it snowed, we played snow cricket. If it rained they played Wii Sport. We had a little makeshift cricket nets area behind the house. Any stray balls ended up in a rather mucky field next to the house, so the boys had an incentive to bowl well and bat better. Glyn's special classes were quite physical, quite fun, and he quickly developed his gross and fine motor skills through sport and games.

My younger son's difficulties were mainly physical, and not really part of a developmental disorder but when the child psychologist pointed us in a different direction for his particular needs, I was already knee-deep in information about autism. NHS waiting lists were long and so eventually we consulted an amazing occupational therapist in Surrey, who gave us very specific programmes to follow.

One of his difficulties lay in the fact that he has incredibly sensitive hearing. It is acute, and his pitch is excellent, but as a result of his dyspraxia he has difficulty in prioritising sound. In a restaurant, for example, he might hear a conversation at the next table, dishes clattering in the kitchen, and muzak playing through a speaker. With all of this going on it is difficult for him to sort out which sounds he should be listening to.

When her report came through the letterbox, I was mystified. It was a completely new language for me. His co-ordination was poor, his memory was poor, his ability to forward plan and organize his thoughts were poor. We knew already about his hyper-sensitive hearing, but she described many sensory difficulties that must have been making his life uncomfortable. Dyspraxia, sensory defensiveness, and the rather wordy proprioceptive bilateral integration difficulties (basically, learning to work your hands and legs simultaneously, independently of each other.)

She recommended exercises and activities to give him the sensory input which he craved. Brushing his skin with a soft brush was one of them. Apparently he was going to enjoy the deep pressure and stimulation of having the soft bristles press against his skin. He was going to love jumping off a sofa into a pile of cushions and have me lie on top of them, pressing him between them. He might like a weighted blanket in bed, to hold him close. He was going to want dark glasses for bright sunlight, and noise-cancelling headphones to block out unwanted ambient noise.

I finally just stopped. Rejected the information. It was all too weird. Brushing my son's arm with a soft brush? What was this? He was the brightest, smartest, cutest little kid and I just blocked the help and advice in the report because I had just finally had too much information, wandered into some strange realm of disability from which I didn't think we were ever going to return. It is symptomatic of autism that too much information can be very overwhelming and sometimes lead to a meltdown. I hadn't yet learned how to take large chunks of information and break them down into smaller more manageable sections. I felt like I had to learn everything, and act on everything, immediately.

I shoved the report in a drawer. I couldn't take any more. I decided to just enjoy my children for who they were and stop looking for trouble.

But rather like the phrase "The jury will disregard this remark", I couldn't really ignore what I'd read, and I began to see the symptoms she was describing in his everyday behaviours. He was sensitive, and his handwriting was poor. He had developed incredible mental maths skills because he found it too difficult to write out sums in math class, but when a teacher asked him to explain, or show, his math process he found it difficult to explain his process. His memory was poor, but he could recreate musical phrases, and remember pitches, with ease.

Finally, I took another sneak peek at the report, tried to read it all over again with an open mind, and just accepted that the world is a weird and wonderful place. To quote Hamlet, "There are more things in heaven and earth, Horatio, than are dreamt of in your philosophy." Finally, I took a deep breath and contacted the OT to ask if there was some way she could create some programmes for us to do at home, up in Wales.

She sent us to a colleague of hers, a fun and energetic young woman, who met with us in a scout hut. The session was so much fun. I watched her work with Glyn and I was dying to leap up and join in the fun as well. She was a gangly tomboy, like a big sister to Glyn, and he laughed and smiled as she took him through a whole series of exercises disguised as games. Each week she came in and transformed the scout hut into what looked like a child's circus. There were brightly coloured tumbling mats, swings, cushions, balls, toys, bouncy nets and slides. It was like having a private playdate in a soft-play centre.

She watched his play carefully, made copious notes, and in the end confirmed that she could post us a programme of work that would help him with everything that had been identified in the report.

I was so relieved that I had ignored my mental block about the work. Her programme was long, intricate, very specific, and so much fun. Glyn took to the work like a duck to water.

Strange as it sounds, the sofa cushions exercise that I'd dismissed as an option in the original report was one of his favourites, even earning itself a nickname: Crashpad. Like many children, he also loved the firm contact of bouncing on a trampoline, and the feeling of flying through the air, so we erected a very large trampoline in the front garden.

He had intricate exercises involving tossing and catching a ball against a wall, and spinning, clapping, and alternating catches at the same time. We filled a bin with bird seed and hid plastic toys in it. He was asked to slide a hand down into the bin, wriggling his fingers down through the seed hunting for the toys. You can imagine how it might feel working your hand through a deep box of seed; it gives your fingers a great workout and improved his fine motor skills.

I actually feel that we over-compensated a bit with the therapy games; he became the most wonderful cricket bowler and batsman, and squash player.

There were mental games too, to help him learn how to organise his thoughts and plan ahead. We learned about comfortable clothing, special types of food, and the joy of headphones, to combat his sensory defensiveness. Our OT gave us a series of child-friendly music discs for Glyn to listen to while he worked. These were *For Therapeutic Listening*, by *Vital Sounds*, and were designed to be playing in the background while he concentrated on something else. The CDs had intentional distortions built into them: perhaps a hissing, or scratching, or warping of the pitch. The idea was that he would be working primarily and listening to the music secondarily. When a distortion occurred he would be distracted from his work by the distortion, and then he needed to train himself to concentrate back on his work and ignore the distortion. It was literally an auditory workout.

Once I broadened my mind to accept this new world of therapy, it was exhilarating. Each morning the classroom was littered with origami animals, jazzy music CDs, science projects, artwork, Christmas decorations or Easter eggs, maps of China, photography from nature walks, and brightly coloured chemistry projects. I completely forgot what I was worried about and embraced alternative home education with relish.

We kept the classroom as tidy as we could manage, but because we had a farmhouse-style kitchen we were able to eat meals in the kitchen and leave classroom projects set up, undisturbed overnight.

For Dylan, we hired a fantastic speech and language therapist who worked with him on *Social Stories* and *Comic Book Conversations.*

These are the dreamchildren of the amazing Carol Gray, an American teacher and author, who has developed methods for teaching social skills to autistic children using visual stories (autistic children are visual learners). Comic Strip Conversations teach language skills using stick figures to show physical and verbal interactions.

This was a whole new world to me, and fascinating; just imagine all of this creativity pouring out of our new little home school 'classroom' on the dining room table. And of course the very first Social Story that the tutor created for our son was all about leaving mainstream for home education.

I thought it might have been confusing for Dylan, the idea of home education. I think he thought he would never see his classmates again. Or maybe that all of the schoolchildren would come up to our house. I could see how this might be very confusing. A well-made Social Story can do so much.

I remembered how grim I had felt when they were still in mainstream education. Some days I would wake up in Militant Parent Mode, ringing the school and scheduling appointments and throwing my weight around in the most unpleasant way. Other days I felt soft, and low, and despairing. I think we were very lucky to have made these discoveries in a small, loving, country school, because a much bigger city school could have been a harsher and crueller environment. A London friend of mine, who was a secondary school teacher at a highly rated public school in the area, confirmed this as well. Our boys had been destined for London schools that were very competitive, and probably less tolerant of the difficulties we were having.

We were now living in a rarefied world of our own making. Life was all about the boys and their education. We worked hard and played hard. I was so proud of the work they were doing, and so grateful for the network of friends, family, and tutors who created this beautiful life for our boys.

9

My Glass Wall Gets a Name

"WELL, THEN YOU CAN'T POSSIBLY be autistic. Autistic people have no imagination. They are too literal. I don't think that you're autistic."

He glanced down at his notebook and scribbled a few notes, then closed the book.

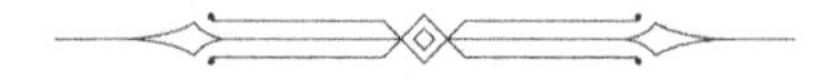

The man I had just seen for my adult autism assessment was a professional. He worked for the NHS. He had been assigned to give me an appointment when I had requested one from my GP. I had a million good reasons why I felt I might be autistic. And yet he sat there smugly, and ever-so-slightly condescendingly, and told me I wasn't autistic. Fuck that.

Here's the thing: imagination isn't empathy. I may lack the ability to "put myself in someone else's shoes", as the popular saying goes, and so yes, I can be crass and insensitive and buy people unsuitable birthday gifts, because I can't imagine what they would really enjoy, and say inconsiderate things to them because I can't second-guess what they might be thinking. And this would be the autism in me. But I also have a fascination for what people think, and why they behave the way that they do, and this curiosity about people and their methods laid the basis for my professional acting, teaching, and directing career.

I found it difficult to understand how I had a career as a professional actress, with such a glaring lack of empathy. Empathy is a key ingredient in an actor's tool kit. This doesn't make sense. I wasn't a brilliant actress – no Oscars on my mantlepiece – but I did work professionally for thirteen years in San Francisco and London, had agents, was member of five professional actors' unions, and taught and directed at a professional actor training school.

I've decided now that because I felt alienated from other people, I enjoyed observing their behaviour from a detached position, and it must have been this ability to observe others that allowed me to recreate their behaviours in my acting work.

When an actor works on a role there are many things he can ask himself about his character in order to make his work believable. Some of the simplest are also the most important. For example, an actor may ask: what does my character want in life? Why does he want it? What does he do to get what he wants? What prevents him getting what he wants, and what does he do as a result? This is a powerful method of working on a role which I learned from Peter, and I realise that I ask myself these questions about people in real life all the time, not just as an actor.

For a brief time, pre-diagnosis, I actually pursued a career in counselling. At the end of the course I wrote to my supervisor and said that I wasn't sure that therapy and counselling were the right fields for me because I "soak up depression like a sponge." *I felt I was too sensitive to be a therapist.*

So welcome to my world. A mass of contradictions.

I stormed around for a bit, like a bear with a sore head. I arranged to see the fantastic psychologist in London, who had diagnosed my son with autism. But at the end of her session she said that she was, by training, a child psychologist, and it was difficult for her to make an accurate assessment without feedback from my parents about my childhood behaviours. I knew nothing about my developmental milestones, and there wasn't anything written down anywhere, that I could see. My parents were both dead. I had never been for a childhood autism assessment, and neither had my father. I'd never even heard about the "A" word until I was in my late thirties, when my son was diagnosed. Asperger's Syndrome was first identified during World War Two, so it had been around a while, but it wasn't mentioned in my little sunshiny Californian upbringing and it was now crashing down on me like a ton of bricks.

I left it a while. Just couldn't bear to continue doggedly pursuing this diagnosis. I can't honestly remember why I tried one last time, but I did in fact finally pick up the bloody phone and arrange yet another appointment for adult autism diagnosis. I hoped and prayed it wouldn't be the same guy. I couldn't remember his name so I decided that if it was a man's name I would cancel and ask for a woman.

As luck would have it, this time it was a woman, albeit in the very same building, and I think quite possibly the very same room. I trusted her immediately; she had no airs or graces. She was blonde and comfortable looking, the sort of woman who would not be out of place on a picnic in the park, or shopping in a garden centre. She wore her skills lightly.

We discussed the difficulties attached to adult diagnosis, and I outlined for her what my son had been through. She treated me like an adult, and an equal. It gave me confidence to feel that I wasn't less of a person, just because I had come to her for a diagnosis.

Without my being aware of it, she began asking about things in my past, and how I felt about them, and how I handled them. I was completely unselfconscious and unguarded; I didn't realise this was part of the assessment. She asked me 'thinking and feeling questions', to get an impression of how I see the world around me and the people in it. She asked me for examples from my life of situations where I felt that autism may have been a cause of conflict with other people.

There was a period in my life when I was ecstatic, and devastated, within a very short space of time. After my father died he left an impressive inheritance for his children. I was given a sum of money which I used to buy a little fisherman's cottage on the coast of Anglesey. I think he would have liked that, being a sailor himself.

I adored this cottage, with fabulous sea views, just three minutes' walk from the water's edge. It was squat and charming, hunkered down next to a vacant lot and looking out towards undeveloped National Trust coastal land. It was in a pretty rundown state and I set to with great passion, turning it into the cottage of my dreams. It used to be just a holiday cottage, but I decided it was going to be our final resting place, and I invested enormously in it, both emotionally and financially.

It's important to choose wisely when buying coastal property, because developers seem to have a habit of squeezing in properties too close to each other, in order to maximise their profits. There were other properties around me but I developed a blinkered approach whereby I could just focus on the dazzling views directly in front of me and try to ignore the comings and goings of my neighbours. My cottage was one of the older properties in the area, surrounded by new-builds of varying quality.

I wanted to find a source of income from home, as Peter was beginning to suffer from a variety of disabilities and needed my care. I decided to open a healthy-option food service from my back garden, providing takeaway meals packed for travel, to supply ramblers on the Anglesey Coastal Path, sailors, and beach day-trippers. There were several holiday lets in the neighbourhood and I wanted to provide catered meals for them as well; it all seemed idyllic.

I didn't want to have table service; I planned for people to order ahead and take away.

I set about my plans, organising a kitchen suitable for commercial food preparation, putting up masking fencing, planning traffic flow, having the inspectors look at my kitchen design. I put in a planning application and sat back, confidently awaiting a positive outcome.

But I failed to consult my neighbours.

It just never crossed my mind. I had decided on this plan, and I had decided that it was a good one, and therefore I didn't even give a thought to how my neighbours might feel. How could anybody object to such a brilliant idea, which worked so well for us personally, and also provided such a wonderful benefit to the local community and tourism industry?

My immediate neighbours were, for the most part, imports from other countries. Three were English, one was South African, and one had been raised in the area but now lived in Buckinghamshire, using her little bungalow less than ten days a year, tops.

The local Welsh population was a warm, loving, generous community, with which I felt a real connection. The ex-pats on the headland, however, were a different sort entirely. They had found their little patch of land, each of them, and defended it to the hilt.

Basic courtesy and politeness on our arrival soon turned to animosity when the planning application went in. Cool personalities turned chilly; one woman actually yelled at me when I went across to introduce myself. I was flummoxed. What was the problem? My business plan solved all of my family's problems, and was sure to be successful; why couldn't my neighbours see that and be supportive?

Because I hadn't told them in detail about my plans – hadn't even introduced myself to some of them properly – they thought the worst. I was thinking salads, soups, yoghurt smoothies and eco-friendly packaging. They were thinking fish and chips, extractor fans, and used pre-portioned ketchup packets littering their front lawns. They decided that I would be offering seating, providing noisy holiday makers with lager, piped-in music, and ash trays for chain-smoking on hot summer evenings.

As I recounted this story in my assessment, I could feel myself getting heated and tearful all over again. I was in such pain, having found my Nirvana, hidden away deep in a pit of vipers.

She looked at me, concerned and slightly bemused.

"Judging from what you've just told me, and your subsequent reaction, I would have to say that, yes, I feel you are definitely on the spectrum. We are all on the spectrum somewhere, everybody, but some more than others. And for those people for whom it is debilitating, then it becomes a problem. You behaved in the way that you did because you couldn't empathise with how your neighbours might feel, and you tried to go ahead with your plans unaware of how others would react to your behaviour."

I felt simultaneously exposed and discovered. She went on to explain, or reframe my anecdote, through the eyes of my neighbours; took the camera that had been filming my version of events and swung it around so that it was a camera filming their version of events. I began to understand what had gone wrong. I was mortified that I hadn't picked up on this instinctively, but also had enough clarity to realise that this blindness, this blinkered behaviour, was symptomatic of recurring problems I had been having my whole life.

I was beginning to nose-dive, but she kept me airborne.

I couldn't figure out how I had found a man who said he loved me, why he had married me, and stayed married to me for all these years. I felt so unlovable. I couldn't figure out why anybody ever spoke to me or called me their friend. I couldn't understand why my children kissed me and hugged me. I felt like such an awful person. I felt so embarrassed that I was such a crass individual. I couldn't understand why students had followed my directing notes, or listened to me in class, and I certainly didn't understand how I had ever got an acting job, if I was such a poor judge of character. How could I understand how a character might behave?

And as for my counselling and therapy work, why did I do so well in the counselling course, and why did they recommend me for a much-coveted work study placement, and why did my friend in my supervision group send me clients to work with? I just had absolutely no idea what was going on.

Actually, on the surface I'm not a very good friend. Peter says you need to make an effort to keep friendships. But just because I don't ring people and talk to them doesn't mean I'm not thinking about them. To me that's a kind of friendship, holding someone in your thoughts.

I feel very connected to Peter and the boys. But I also have a friend. In London. Susan is the parent of one of Glyn's classmates from nursery school and we've corresponded on and off for decades. Sometimes we don't write for months, and then suddenly it's a flurry of activity for days. We share the same sense of humour. She reminds me of my mum, what my mum would have grown into had she not fallen ill. Both of them very understated and funny and devout… and good Christians.

I guess sometimes in life you just have to wing it, blindly, until the fog clears. I decided that it was what it was – my history was my history – and I couldn't change it, but I could get on with my life with the insights I'd been given. And most importantly, cut myself some slack about my lack of empathy. I mean, I was still going to make mistakes, I was still going to behave without empathy from time to time, I was still going to crash through peoples' sensitivities like a bull in a china shop.

If the Autism Fairy waved her magic wand over me one day and made me neuro-typical, what fun I would have! I would be able to walk into a room and sense that Peter just wanted some quiet time, rather than barging in and asking him to do some little nagging chore that I wanted done. I would let people queue jump in a shop when clearly they were in a hurry, rather than calling them on it as a point of principle. I wouldn't mind a bit if a friend coming to stay changed her plans for the fourth time, because I would now be a very patient and understanding person, and when she cancelled her visit altogether because of work I would be delighted for her and reach for the calendar, smiling graciously, to re-schedule.

I would go out more, to noisy places like pubs and live concerts and crowded cafés during the lunch hour. I would be able to wear tight fitting blue jeans with a belt, and woollen jumpers next to my skin. I would never glare at smokers. I would empathise with people who told me they were not feeling well, instead of feeling inwardly annoyed that our plans had to be cancelled. I would make a habit of performing charitable good deeds, because I would no longer resent working for no pay.

Oh, what a marvellous person I would be!

I'm not. I'm me: grouchy, moody, impulsive, unreasonable, petty, pig-headed, inflexible. But the people who have stayed with me all these years must know me by now, and if they don't want to be around me they won't be. What else can I do?

10

Our Legacy

I THINK BACK OVER THE childhoods of my father, myself, and my sons, from an autistic perspective.

Our boys have been so lucky.

My father was a brilliant, lonely, only child. After his parents divorced and his adored mother died of leukaemia, his father re-married – a woman with a room entirely dedicated to her pet cats – and she eventually gambled away his family's rather extensive fortune.

Asperger's Syndrome was unknown when he was a boy. He just had to figure it out and cope with it all on his own. His love of numbers, and chemistry, allowed him to take control of his life.

He was happy and safe with his maths and his science and his wonderful wife and his elegant little sailing boat, three children, two dogs, and a sprawling ranch style home, complete with swimming pool, in the Californian hills outside of L.A.

Not a bad outcome for a kid on the spectrum.

As for me, beneath the veneer of a happy childhood I was very anxious. When I was small, I had a curious habit of running to the window whenever my mother drove off to the shops, staring fixedly out of the window after her until I couldn't see her anymore. I was preoccupied with the thought that it might be the last time I ever saw her alive. I began to have daily stomach aches every morning before school – classic school phobia – and I was finally taken in for tests to see if I had developed an ulcer.

I used to ride the school bus each morning and afternoon, a long slow diesel-fuelled ascent from my Junior High School up towards our home in the hills of La Canada. One day the typical teenage messing about in the back of the bus got so noisy, the driver stopped the bus and refused to continue with the route until order had been restored.

This was horrific for me. I felt trapped. I couldn't breathe. I had a panic attack. When we finally started up again I got off at the next stop and ran the rest of the way home. I never rode that bus again. Each day it was a long run or half-walk, half-run to school as quickly as I could.

Like many children, I just thought that things like this had to be endured. I thought it was the price of growing up. It never occurred to me that things could be different. My inner child and my outer child were at odds with each other.

But of course I had also grown up in that very same, very privileged world that my father created for us. Eventually I became an actor, and when we moved to the coast, I was very active in all areas of the drama department and the music department, took on little part-time jobs in fast food restaurants, and went to the beach. A lot.

But as my mother's illness worsened, I began to feel that seismic shift in the relationships with the people around me.

My father was a no-go area. He was fragile as glass; I couldn't reach him. Or perhaps, he couldn't reach me.

From an autistic perspective, this was not good. Apparently, girls are better able to conceal signs of autism, and I tried my best not to be the difficult child. Not acting out was the kindest thing I could possibly have done for my parents at this time.

I think they were waiting for me to cause trouble.

I never did.

At the time in life when most teenagers were pushing the boundaries of their relationships with their parents, and finding new mentors outside of the family circle to model themselves on, I was hanging on for dear life because my mother was dying. I didn't look for freedom, I craved closeness. Growing up and leaving became a death sentence, not an aspiration.

I didn't realise then, that the death of a parent, to an autistic child, pushes the worst possible buttons in terms of security, confidence, and connection. And my father was paralysed with grief. I think if you could dream up the worst possible life changing event to send to my father, it would've been the slow, lingering death of his wife.

She had been the conduit through which my father coped with the outside. She interpreted Life for him.

Now, not only was he a grieving husband, he was a grieving parent as well. He did what he did best: he concentrated on making a secure financial future for us all. He felt emotionally safe when he was financially safe, with his facts and figures and accounts books and his calculator, and his Bourbon and Coke on the rocks, and it was the way he expressed his love for us, and the way he honoured the memory of my mother.

But in terms of emotional support, he just wasn't there. He couldn't be. His mouthpiece, his interpreter, was dead. He just didn't have the vocabulary.

If you've ever driven a car with wet brakes, you'll know how difficult it can be. Maybe you're putting your foot on the brakes – but you're hydroplaning – and the brakes don't work at all, and your car carries on at speed, out of control. Or maybe you put your foot lightly on the brakes, but the car slams to a stop abruptly. Wet brakes. That was me, for years, trying to learn how to let go.

It's incredibly ironic that one of the major stumbling blocks for me in life – my poor maths skills – was my father's crowning glory. He was just so smart. He graduated top of his class with a master's degree in chemical engineering from the California Institute of Technology. He was quickly head-hunted into a senior position with an oil company.

And yet I inherited none of this. Not only do I not have a neuro-typical brain, I also don't have some of the positive qualities commonly associated with autism.

People on the spectrum can be excellent musicians and composers. I love music, and at one point in my life had planned on a career as a professional musician. So that makes sense. But when it came to composition my brain went into overload. That didn't make sense. I can read music but I can't create a musical score. I know now that my brain doesn't create the mathematical structures required to compose. So I guess you could say I respond to the creative element in music, but not the analytical element required to compose it.

My father recognised that I had these difficulties but didn't have the communication skills required to help. He could only think in one particular way, and although he tried, he couldn't find a way to access my way of thinking and help me with maths and science.

My personal challenge as a parent is equally profound. I was an atypical autistic mother, raising an atypical autistic child, in a neurotypical world. And our youngest son, with his different set of challenges, was living with an autistic mother and an autistic sibling and having to negotiate all that that entailed. I went through a long period where I didn't trust my instincts at all.

I have struggled for years with the natural process of watching my boys grow up and become independent. I have been told how it all works. I have seen a smooth transition from other parents. I understand intellectually how it works. I just find it hard, so hard, to let go, myself.

Concealing problems from my parents became a skill and a habit, and from an autistic perspective was the worst thing I could have done. Children do their best to learn coping mechanisms, with their limited, adolescent understanding, and sometimes it can take years to undo the more unhelpful of these mechanisms. But as far as I know the word autism was unheard of in my childhood home, and it took an entire generation to pass before the "A" word appeared in my life, through my sons.

So yes, Dylan and Glyn have been lucky. The specialist tutors and bouncy balls and Social Stories and cricket and home school and headphones have all come from adoring parents who want to give them the best start in life. Armed with our new knowledge of autism, I think we have. They're not stupid. I'm not stupid. We are very clever, but in a different way. I hope one day we can have a sort of shorthand between us.

11

Coming Up for Air

COUNTRY LIFE REALLY SUITS ME. I love the quiet. There was a period where we moved around quite a lot, and each house moved us progressively closer to our neighbours, and towards town life.

Finally, we overstepped the mark. We bought an ancient Italian townhouse, with neighbours above, below, across, and to either side of us. Inside, the house was as calm and elegant as a cathedral, but everything in the street was made of stone, and noise pinged off of the walls like a laser. Culturally, Italians are notoriously expressive, and every day the village echoed with the sounds of radios, hoovers, birds, dogs, Vespas, and the gregarious interactions of my neighbours.

Here in Wales, most days it's peaceful, punctured only occasionally by sheep-related farming activity from our neighbour.

I have a very noisy mind. I think that's why I crave quiet. I don't know if other people have noisy minds as well; I've got nothing to compare it to. I just know that I'm always thinking about something, over-thinking about something, obsessing about something, worrying about something. When I'm travelling I don't read to pass the time. I'd much rather look out of the window of a car, or train, or plane, and think about things, and people watch. One summer I spent days on end in my bedroom, sitting on the floor reading

The Hobbit, and my dad came in and told me I was wasting my summer reading, when I should have been outdoors enjoying my vacation. He was right, of course, but if you've ever got stuck into a great book, real life pales in comparison, even at the seaside in California. Actually, I don't read very much anymore. I can't concentrate on long books for some reason. So it's pretty weird that I've started writing.

I'll tell you my take on autism: it's a blessing and it's a curse. I learned from watching my son work with his speech and language therapist that so much insight which is lacking in an autistic person can be taught. These things may be things that a neurotypical person would pick up instinctively, and an autistic person might not, but through the aforementioned *Social Stories*, and *Comic Strip Conversations*, social skills can be taught. And empathy can be learned, albeit usually after the fact.

But in my opinion the curse of autism is this: because it is a developmental disorder, an autistic person will continually be growing, and changing, and just when one developmental lesson might be learned, then a new one comes along, and the autistic person is again drowning in a sea of confusion. A new wave of experience. Drowning him.

So life becomes one long struggle to learn the neurotypical behaviours appropriate for your age and society. And then the next ones. And then the next ones. And perhaps the information that you finally learned about how to behave as you were supposed to have done last year is now out of date, and a new set of behaviours must be learnt. I find myself, even today at the ripe age of 61, acting-out teenage behaviours that I never allowed myself when I was actually a teenager, because at that time too much other really hefty stuff was coming down, and teenage acting-out didn't really seem appropriate.

No one ever promised us a smooth ride, neuro-typical or atypical. And it's impossible to protect yourself from making blunders. I guess the secret is not minding. And learning from your mistakes. And forgiving yourself.

12

My Guardian of the Glass

AUTISM IS VERY FRIGHTENING AND very lonely. Every thought or belief I have had as a parent, I have questioned, so worried was I about my faulty "emotional compass". It must've been exhausting for Peter, having to wade daily through my chronic worry with me, sort out the real problems from the imaginary ones, and give me a sense of perspective which I was innately lacking.

I haven't written much about him. Therefore you might be curious about who this man so deserving of a medal might be. He is stocky and kindly, with a full head of salt-and-pepper hair and a warm smile. It's very difficult to write about him, without being cringy. He's just such a lovely man.

We've been married for over thirty years; I'm twenty years his junior. We come from completely different worlds. If you ask him he will tell you about his wartime, and post-war life, a childhood filled with Bakelite restaurant tokens, rationing, and a beloved dog named Patch. He was born in Kent, and so he's a "Kentish Man" because he was born west of the river Medway. A "Man of Kent" would be born to the east. It's just possible that these two terms are interchangeable....

I've no idea where Peter's acting background comes from; his family was in the motor trade. His parents were always very kind when we went to visit, and if they had any qualms about him marrying a tall blonde American from California, they never showed it.

I think I was only ever in disgrace once with his parents. Once during a visit, we had been having a jovial discussion about meat pies over a full proper Devon Sunday lunch. I bragged about a new recipe I had unearthed, for veal and ham pie, and in the way that one tosses out promises in the heat of the moment, I promised them a homemade pie on our next visit, and then promptly forgot all about it.

Sadly, they did not, and in a few months' time, as we arrived round about supper time, I saw the table smartly laid out for supper, and they saw me emerge from the car with flowers, but no food. With true British grace, defrosting ensued, and I just had to sit there feeling bad, until I felt better.

I'm not sure what we have in common, but it doesn't matter because it works. The vast difference in our backgrounds is part of the fun. We still crease up at each other's jokes and find deep companionship in each other's company as well as each other's silences.

He will tell you that I chatted him up, at a lecture he was giving in San Francisco. I will vehemently deny it. I went up after the lecture to ask him a legitimate question about drama training, and I stand by my story.

13

The Incarnations

I'VE READ THAT THE ONE thing all autism sufferers have in common is that no two are alike. Cheeky little phrase, but it's actually true. Many autistic people are maths superstars, like my father. Many are computer experts. And yet many are maths deficient, like me.

I've had many incarnations over the years; some better than others. I think the members of my family smile whenever I confront them with a new career idea. I am gently teased about this, but no one really appreciates that when I am in the throes of visualising another career path, it seems like a really good idea at the time.

I was going to buy and run a pub in Cheshire. I was going to run corporate retreats out of a historic lighthouse on Anglesey. I was going to run bed and breakfast out of a Georgian vicarage in Eglwysbach. I was going to host music concerts for children with disabilities. There was the catering idea, the travel blogging, the drama school in Cardiff, the cricket academy, the cookery school in Italy. My face is hot and flushed and I'm embarrassed about the things I have tried to accomplish.

I actually did run children's drama classes for a while, in Bala, but handed over the work when we decided to home educate. I had worked as a professional actor in America, and in London, and had taught and directed drama students for thirteen years, so I knew what I was doing. When I set up the programme I was anticipating teaching the classes myself. But the local community thought otherwise: they wanted me to administrate in American, and have a local drama teacher teach the classes in Welsh. So I didn't actually end up doing what I wanted to do, what I was experienced at doing: teaching and directing. But it seemed a popular programme, the kids liked it, and the local teacher was great with children of all ages.

I love the plays of Anton Chekhov. He's such a keen observer of behaviour. Like an onion, you can always peel away another layer in a Chekhov play. He was first and foremost a man of science, a doctor, but he was such an artist as well. I think that's incredible.

Here was a man who lived a life full of writing, theatre, and costumes and opening night parties, and yet he took time out to travel all the way across Russia in order to observe and write about prison reform on Sakhalin Island, a grim and unbearable penal colony on the Eastern coast of Russia.

He wrote about the lightness, and darkness, in all of us.

I think it's difficult for Western European actors to latch on to Russian humour. That incredible ability to laugh, and then to cry, in the same sentence. The best example of Russian humour I've seen recently is in the film *The Death of Stalin*, and perhaps *Hotel Budapest.* I find it very difficult myself, when directing a scene, but I love it when I see it.

I used to love directing Chekhov scenes with young actors, but I don't work in the theatre anymore. I would teach them to really dig down and look at the questions that Peter said were so important in characterisation: What does your character want? How does he go about getting what he wants? What prevents him getting what he wants? What does he do instead?

I used to apply these questions to counselling as well. Because the questions we ask of our characters are really the same questions we ask of people in real life.

I can't tell if I'm eccentric or not. I know I'm not purple-hair eccentric, but maybe I'm quietly eccentric, quirky, maybe. I have no idea how I come across to other people. If I was asked to describe myself I wouldn't have a clue where to begin. I guess I'd say people thought I was funny, but I'm not sure if that's funny-ha ha-funny, or funny-weird-funny. I have an odd sense of humour, but then I think if you ask most people they would say they have an odd sense of humour.

At university I could be very overt, spraying my hair black for parties and wearing weird clothes, but I think that's typical. Now I have very boring conservative clothing that is soft and loose, and I rarely wear makeup or jewellery, and I'm frustratingly overweight but feel helpless to do anything about it, because I have no discipline, no structure, no will power. So many things have fallen by the wayside for me, as just not being very important anymore. But I need to discover what is important, and that I'm not very sure about yet.

I used to have big obsessions that would last for months, or even years, and also little skirmishes of obsessions that might last only for a day or two. Little obsessions might be a sudden fascination with old Roman roads, or the migration of language across Western Europe, or the history of ancient Doggerland. These are things that weren't part of my education in California so I'm sort of catching up on British and European history now that I live here.

I'm passionate about houses, architecture, colour, and interior design. Whenever we are looking for a new place to live it consumes me for days, or even weeks, trawling through property listings, and even when we find the perfect new house, I still continue to trawl, just to make sure I haven't missed anything.

I'm writing, now. I hope it sticks. It seems to suit me.

EPILOGUE

DYLAN IS NOW A DISABILITY sport cricket coach at Old Trafford in Manchester. He organises in-school and extra-curricular cricket clubs, in and around the Manchester area. He was lucky in his early cricket experiences. The Welsh coaches he grew up with had a gentle, informal, nurturing style of coaching, and this is reflected in his own work. No shouting, no alpha behaviours, no blood-thirsty competitive edge. It was a very healthy environment. Luckily, the head of the Junior coaching division at his club worked in Special Needs, and really took Dylan under his wing: worked through the temper flare-ups, safeguarded him from bullying, taught him about coping with the fairness, and unfairness, of the sporting world. He achieved a degree in Sport Coaching at Cardiff Met and has used that qualification to great advantage in his work. He is happiest with a bat or ball in his hand. On rainy days, when he feels cooped up, he prowls the house like a caged lion, air batting and air bowling at imaginary opponents.

Glyn studied Maths, and then changed to Civil Engineering, at Cardiff University, but as nearly every waking moment was spent with his guitar, he is now carving out a niche for himself as a singer and guitarist instead. He's branching out into composition, jazz improvisation, and beginning to record his own work with a view to posting it online, and busking. Walk past his bedroom door and you can hear jazzy licks, tender ballads, creative noodling, and a truly lovely singing voice.

Writing has opened me up. It's like someone has put a tap on the side of my Wall of Glass, and turned it on, and all of these thoughts and feelings now come pouring out of the spout. Writing allows me to communicate, but from a distance. I can write something down and have a look at it and really think about whether or not that's what I want to say, rather than verbally being tactless or unthinking or impulsive. I feel safer writing personal stuff, rather than saying it. I don't have to look people in the face and I don't get distracted by their facial expressions.

Peter and I are still testing the waters to see what life looks like with grown up children. We have moved home a lot and travelled frequently, even living in Italy for nearly a year. Our lives are constructed of two imaginary elastic bands. One is wrapped around ourselves and our children. The other is wrapped around ourselves and Wales. If we stray too far, the bands pull us back, and back we come willingly. These are not the ties that bind. These are the ties of love.

Marcie Layton, June 2021

Marcie Layton

Marcie Layton is a memoirist, living in North Wales. She writes about Wales, her family, travel in Italy, and her experience of life on the autistic spectrum. Previously published work includes 'Fy, i'r Dinosaur', in the short story anthology *Tales of Independence and Belonging*, published by Parthian books.

Photo: Andrew Nash

Printed in Great Britain
by Amazon